£3-50

D1493239

Blyth, Greene, Jourdain
and Company Limited
1810–1960

Thomas Blyth, 1765–1839, founder of the firm,
from a painting in the London board room

Blyth, Greene, Jourdain & Company Limited 1810-1960

by Augustus Muir

NEWMAN NEAME

Published for
BLYTH, GREENE, JOURDAIN
AND COMPANY LIMITED
PLANTATION HOUSE, FENCHURCH STREET, LONDON EC3
by
NEWMAN NEAME LIMITED
LONDON, BIRMINGHAM AND MANCHESTER
and printed in Great Britain at
THE CURWEN PRESS LIMITED
LONDON E I 3

FOREWORD

*It was decided in 1959 to publish a brief History
of Blyth, Greene, Jourdain and Company Limited in
connection with the celebration in 1960 of the 150th
anniversary of its foundation. The destruction, however, of
almost all the Company's archives in the air raid
of 10th May 1941, made the task long and difficult;
consequently publication has been greatly delayed.
The business has always been a family business and it
has been possible to make use of many extracts taken from
family records concerning its early years. As regards more recent
times, we are grateful to all those who have provided
information about events occurring within their own memories.
Mr Augustus Muir, the author, carried out a great deal
of research on his own account. In addition he has
made very good use of the material submitted to him.
Our special thanks are due to him
for the great skill and care with which he has put
together the interesting story contained in this book.*

M. FORTESCUE-BRICKDALE

PLATES

FRONTISPIECE
Thomas Blyth, 1765–1839, founder of the firm

FACING PAGE 9
The first entry in the daybook of Thomas Blyth,
Sons and Company

FACING PAGE 12
Invoice for part of the first shipment of sugar made by
Thomas Blyth, Sons and Company

FACING PAGE 16
The poop deck of the *Isabella Blyth*

FACING PAGE 19
Lieutenant Gordon's cabin on the *Isabella Blyth*

FACING PAGE 20
Portraits of James Blyth, Henry D. Blyth and Benjamin Buck Greene

FACING PAGE 27
The *Sea Breeze*, one of the fleet of 'pea-soupers'

FACING PAGE 38
Letter from Mr Muhlinghaus of the Borneo Company to
Samuel Gilfillan and his partners

FACING PAGE 42
Port Louis in 1842, showing the *Isabella Blyth* arriving
and the *Thomas Blyth* leaving

CONTENTS

9
The Blyths of Limehouse

12
The Island Trader

16
The Thomas Blyth, *First of the Merchantmen*

19
A New Partnership

21
Mauritius and London

25
The Incorporation of the Company (1894)

28
Expansion in Three Continents

34
Changes in Mauritius

38
The Malayan Establishment

42
The Second World War

47
New Spheres of Influence

53
The Company Today

55
Appendix
Companies in the Group at 31st December 1960

Port Louis Mauritius 15th Sep.r 1830

Received of B.S. Houghton a cheque						
on Bosanquets on the 4th June at Portsmouth						
just previous to departure and handed down						
to Ins. Bettington Sons &c — p. Mr Bettington						
Sen.r to be carried to Credit of our Account £9.2.1 Stg.				45	57	

Received pr Orontes 4 Cases cont.g

Sundry Coins of which 2 Cases opened

containing as under

1603 Gold Doubloons	5557.1.4	27785	33¼		
272 S. Dollars	58.18.8	294	66¾		
1 Mex — .. —	4	1	.		
260 A. Rupees	24.18.4	124	58¼		
150/. S. Dollars	32.11.1	162	77		
102 9/8 Pieces	20.8.—	102	.		
12 7/. Doubloons	44.12.8	223	17	28693	52

20

Paid Cash

B.S. Houghton for a cheque rec.d of him at Portsmouth	45	57
a acc.t of Sundry Coins being B.S.Houghton proportion		
of gain on 5 ————————	3	11	48	68

21

Paid Cash

Servants onboard the Orontes for B.lk ————	20	11
Landing Sundries from d.o — articles on Trade Acc.t —	14	.	34	.

Oct.r 1st

Paid Cash

Sundry Articles purchased for use of Trade at a Sale

by Auction of the Effects of the late M. Mallet

1 Counting House Table with Railing, Pigeon Holes, Boxes &c —	42	.
1 Large Bookcase part glazed	42	.
1 d.o Table with Drawers	22	25
	106	25
Auction duty 2p% 2..12 Porterage 1.—	3	12	109	37

18

Paid Cash

a acc.t of Trade Expences Rent of Premises 1st. inst.			60	.

The first entry in the daybook of Thomas Blyth, Sons and Company, dated 15th September 1830

CHAPTER ONE

The Blyths of Limehouse

T HOMAS BLYTH, the founder of the firm, was born on 14th October 1764, and his marriage to Isabella Forster took place in 1793 at the church of St George-in-the-East in the parish of Stepney. It is impossible to say whether he was born and brought up in Stepney, for the relevant parish records were destroyed during the blitz on London in the second world war, as were the early archives of Blyth, Greene, Jourdain and Company. Among members of one branch of Thomas Blyth's descendants, there is a tradition that the family came south from Northumberland or Berwickshire. Another tradition locates the family at Kirkcaldy in Fife; certainly, Thomas Blyth's sister, Allison, was married to a Kirkcaldy man, William Scotland.

We come to safer ground when we say that in 1810 Thomas Blyth became the owner of a large wharf and adjacent premises at 45 Fore Street (now part of Narrow Street) in Limehouse, and he set up in business as a sail-maker and ship chandler under the style of Thomas Blyth and Company. Later he extended his business to include coopering, oil-sanding, and the making of whaling gear; he had shares in a number of South Seas whalers (one of them was named the *Eliza Anne*) and he traded in sperm oil. He had a skilled eye for the lines and equipment of a ship, and in all likelihood had once been a ship's master. Of his eldest son, Thomas, a poet, we know little; but both his second and third sons, Henry David and James, he took into partnership in 1826, and the firm of Thomas Blyth and Sons was formed. Henry had become a member of the Joiners' Company in 1821, and was to be his father's right-hand man for many years. A few doors away from the Blyths' wharf and premises, his two youngest sons, John and Alfred, set up in business as engineers.

Thomas Blyth's fourth son, Philip, seems to have had plenty of enterprise but little business ability. Twice the young man was given a chance to prove himself, but both times with unfortunate results. The thoughts of Thomas Blyth then turned to Mauritius as a possible venue for Philip's energies. The French flag had flown there for nearly a century before British troops had landed on the island during the Napoleonic Wars and captured it. Since 1810, under British governors, its prosperity had quickly grown; and inside less than two decades under the new rule, five times more sugar was being exported than ever before. In the course of a long voyage, James Blyth had visited Mauritius and on his return to London his father and he had resolved to establish a business house there with James himself as its moving spirit. Before this project had materialised, however, Thomas Blyth decided to give Philip another chance to make good, and the young man sailed for Mauritius with ten thousand pounds at his disposal.

On reaching Port Louis, Philip Blyth fell into the hands of a Captain Bébé Lesage, who, many years before, had been ADC to Sir Robert Townsend Farquhar, the first British Governor of Mauritius, and impulsively he entered into partnership with the old man. In fact, Lesage's business was in deep water and it was Philip's handsome contribution that kept it afloat. Without concern for the consequences, Philip drew bills on the family firm in Limehouse, and Thomas Blyth soon realised that something was far wrong. Conferring with his two sons, he decided to put into operation the project they had often talked of – namely, the formation of an associated firm in Mauritius – and James sailed for the island without delay to establish this subsidiary business and to look into Philip's affairs. In conjunction with some members of the Bettington family (one of whom was a trader in Australia) the Mauritius firm of Thomas Blyth, Sons and Company was formed on 21st May 1830, and James arrived on the island four months later.

It did not take him long to discover that Philip had recklessly put his name to more than two thousand bills for various amounts, payable at different dates during the next seven years; and worse still, even after Philip had realised that Captain Lesage had misled him, he had continued to draw bills on the family firm in London for large sums. James commented sharply on 'the imprudent conduct Philip exhibited here in so seriously involving so much property not his own, which might have effected the ruin of our whole family'. In addition, Philip had involved not only the family firm but two good friends of his father's – Captain C. A. Harris and Francis Whiting. The latter was active in business in London and was a proprietor of the Phoenix Assurance Company. In conjunction with these two gentlemen, the Blyths of Limehouse had been owners of the sailing ship, *Amelia Wilson*, which had arrived at Mauritius with a valuable cargo. Foolishly, Philip had arranged for Captain Bébé Lesage to handle it, but because of his being already in difficulties the proceeds could not be paid to the owners of the ship.

James Blyth found the position to be extremely complicated, and he reckoned that Thomas Blyth and Sons would lose over £3,000. However, James discovered that the

Lesage firm had advanced over £20,000 to the owner of a rather dilapidated sugar estate of 700 acres, and as it was the only Lesage asset he at once obtained a mortgage on it. On Bon Accueil, as it was called, there was a mansion house and ninety slaves, reckoned to be worth £80 each. This shrewd move was to be the saving of the situation created by his brother, who was made bankrupt and by law could not leave the colony until his affairs had been put in order. It had not taken James Blyth long to see what type of man Captain Lesage was. Acting on questionable legal advice, Lesage tried to get the mortgage deed nullified; but after the affair had dragged on for four years in the local court, the verdict was in James Blyth's favour. He foreclosed on the mortgage, then sent to London for Captain Harris to come out to run the estate, and this was done so profitably over several years that he eventually sold it at a price that fully recompensed the London House and his father's two friends, Captain Harris and Francis Whiting. James Blyth was a good brother to Philip, but nothing which happened in Mauritius did anything to improve his opinion of him as a man of business.

CHAPTER TWO

The Island Trader

HEN JAMES had arrived at Port Louis on the *Orontes* in September 1830, he had brought with him from London a considerable quantity of specie to finance his operations on the island – doubloons, Spanish pillar dollars, Mexican dollars, Sicca rupees and other coins accepted as currency in Mauritius. As his right-hand man he had taken with him Benjamin Houghton, who was to prove a loyal servant of the firm. In his office in Port Louis, James worked late and early, beginning at six o'clock in the morning and continuing far on into the evening. Before long his staff had increased to half a dozen, and he was writing home:

'The more I look at the present position of our affairs, the more I am of the opinion that this House, under good management, will make all of us a fortune.'

The number of vessels to its agency was continually increasing, and he imported for sale an immense variety of goods – canvas, crockery, gunpowder, beer, linseed oil, copper, nails, seaming twine, Jamaican coffee, sheet lead, deals, planks and bricks. He sold much of this himself by auction, and reported that 'the sales of no other Houses go off with such spirit as ours'.

He was not always so ebullient; there were moments when he could not banish the nostalgia that came over him and he longed to be back home again in England. In a letter to his brother Henry he wrote:

'This place does not agree with my wife. . . . But we are determined to endure all discomforts in the hope that a few years may enable us to return to England with enough to live on quietly. When I set off from England, £1,500 a year was what I regarded as the Independence for which I was to work. Twelve months ago, I got down to £1,000, and I have been diminishing it to £500, where I suppose I must stop – unless indeed I were to tell you the truth that I hate the place so much that £200 a year in a cheap part of England or Scotland would be preferable to me than the Governor's allowance of £10,000 a year here. However, as I am in for it, and I have no doubt

Invoice of 3382 Bags Mauritius Sugars, shipped on the Amelia Wilson Cap. E. Allen by Thos. Blyth Sons &Co. Port Louis & consigned for Sale to Thos. Bottington Sons &Co. London

			Gross	Tare	Nett			$	C.s
⬦ B 2.2 J.M.Bus	146	Bags	16741	3 p %	16239	@ $2.75 p %		446	56
⬦ B 31 No.1	60	"	8162	3½	7877	3.00	236 31		
" 21 Dargno	100	"	13902	"	13416		402 48		
" 33 Reeves	75	"	9588	3	9301	"	279 03		
" 32 Brue	35	"	4597	3½	4437	"	133 17		
" 21 Jeanne Mauricent	33	"	3725	3	3614	"	108 42	1159	41
" 1	65	"	6225	3	6039	$3.25	196 26		
" J Dauchigny	55	"	4700	3	4559	"	148 16		
" 14	155	"	17862	3	17326	"	563 09		
" 12	183	"	25998	3½	25089	"	815 39	1722	90
" 11 Rivier Lanivin	215	"	26975	3	26166	} 3 3/4		1761	65
" "	216	"	26975	3½	26031				
" 24 Jeanne Mauricent	41	"	4930	3	4783	3.50	167 41		
" 13 T	162	"	19835	3	19250	}			
" 23 T	133	"	16093	3	15611	}	1219 75		
" 4	260	"	31286	3½	30191		1056 68		
" 43	188	"	22901	3	22214		777 49	3221	33
" 44	356	"	47998	3½	46318	3 7/8		1679	02
" 42 A	444	"	52935	3½	51083	3 ¾		1915	60
								11906	47
					Cash 6 p Ct dist			714	38
								11792	09
" 34 A	280	"	62533	3	60658	at 3.05 cash		1850	06	13042 15
	3382								

Charges

Customs Duties	1026	06
Quay Dues	70	46
Tonnage &c	48	45
Lighterage	74	95
Cartage	174	50
Charcoal & marking	7	50
Brokerage	68	78
	1470	70
	$14512	85

DB 29

Invoice for part of the first shipment of sugar made by Thomas Blyth, Sons and Company. The shipment left Mauritius on 20th January 1831 in the Amelia Wilson

that our object will be fully answered by patience and perseverance, I shall content myself with things as they are, and fag as hard as I do, and as hard as I have done since coming here, in the hope that by 1840 you and I will both have enough to settle down quietly with. If we have not, it will not be for want of proper diligence and industry on your part or mine.'

But these moods were evanescent and did not check his ardour in business. By 1833 his father and brother in London were shipping goods to him at the rate of £20,000 per annum.

'Representatives of other Houses,' he wrote home, 'have asked how we could send to England for such immense quantities of goods and sell them off on arrival at prices apparently below prime cost. The whole secret is that you buy, pack, freight out, etc, so cheaply that we can beat them out of the field.'

Success was coming to him surely and steadily in spite of the difficulties he had to face. His own prosperity was largely tied up with that of the planters, and he saw that in a short time a situation might arise in which the financial stability of the island would be shaken.

For some time the use of slave labour had been a lively topic of dispute. The Governor of Mauritius, Sir Charles Colville, had been ordered by Whitehall to abolish the official colour bar, and the coloured people had become excited at the prospect of their sharing some of the amenities enjoyed by the white population. When Mauritius had belonged to France, the Republican Government – pledged to 'liberty, fraternity and equality' – had freed all slaves in the French Empire; but the Mauritian planters had stoutly refused to obey, and the island had virtually ruled itself for a time as an independent French colony. Since those French planters had successfully disobeyed a decree from Paris, they and their sons saw no reason why they should obey the British Government. They were led by Adrien d'Epinay, a successful planter and now a politician. In the post of Procureur Général, the Governor had replaced d'Epinay's brother by John Jeremie, who favoured the freeing of the slaves, and most people believed that this would bring ruin on them all. Under Adrien d'Epinay's leadership, there was an immediate strike. Shopkeepers, barristers, Government servants, dock workers and many others refused to carry on with their normal tasks. There was even a threat of armed resistance. This agitation at first met with some success, and Sir Charles Colville capitulated and agreed to send John Jeremie back to England. As a result, a new Governor, Sir William Nicolay, was appointed and additional troops were sent out from England to help to preserve the peace and enforce the law.

It was impossible for James Blyth to stand aside from this storm. In 1832, we find him writing to his brother in London: 'There is not a more liberal minded and generous set of men than the planters in Mauritius, but a few agitators keep them constantly on the fret.' It was only twenty-two years since the British had taken over the island and no doubt James Blyth felt, with other Englishmen at this time, that British rule in the colony would be endangered if able French patriots such as Adrien d'Epinay could not be restrained. James Blyth felt so strongly about the need for a firm hand in Mauritius that he accepted nomination by Sir William Nicolay as a member of the Legislative Council of Government, and he was the first 'unofficial' Englishman to be so honoured.

❋ ❋ ❋

In Britain, there was widespread assent to the persistent cry that slaves should be freed. The Anti-Slavery Society urged the Government to release the seventy thousand slaves of Mauritius (they formed seven-tenths of the island's population) without compensation to the slave-owners. Since most of the planters and traders were French, they had less influence in London than the slave-owners of the West Indies, and Mauritius was made the thin end of the wedge. With his usual forethought, James Blyth took precautions to prevent the firm being hit hard if a depression in the island's trade should follow abolition of slavery – and he knew abolition to be inevitable. In 1833, the British Government passed the Act that freed all slaves in the Empire, and on 1st February 1835 a new régime began.

The slaves then became paid 'apprentices' and at the end of four years were free to go if they wished. Half of them left the plantations; and to fill the gap, indentured labour was brought from India. The flow increased to such an extent that Indians were one day to form the majority of the island population. Even before the end of the four-year period, James Blyth had been sending vessels to Bengal to bring back labourers and cargoes of the rice that was their staple food.

The Mauritian planters had reckoned that their slaves had been worth about four million pounds. They were in fact allotted just over two of the twenty millions voted by the Government to compensate all slave-owners in British colonies for the loss of eight hundred thousand slaves, of whom seven-eighths were in the West Indies. The compensation was paid in the form of debentures, and in Mauritius these were negotiated by a number of the recognised business houses. Before the competitive rush began for the handling of the debentures, James Blyth wrote to his brother in London giving a list of claims and asked him to send specie in a fast-sailing vessel so that he could have hard cash ready sooner than any other firm on the island. These debentures were payable in Whitehall, and their collection in London on behalf of the Mauritian slave-owners was lucrative. By the beginning of the following year, James

Blyth's profit from the Slave Indemnity Department was £25,000, with more business of the same kind to follow. In the event, few of the Mauritian firms handled more Indemnity debentures than the Blyths.

If the Indemnity brought profit, it also brought trouble to James Blyth. He had been asked to serve on the Slave Indemnity Commission; and over planters' claims, which were based on the number of slaves they legally owned, he had bitter disputes with other members of the Commission:

'My worthy brethren seemed to wish to shut their eyes to the 46th Clause of the Bill put there expressly by Parliament to meet the illegally registered cases . . . I must either falsify my oath or resist the faction.'

He resisted – and resigned from the Commission. He had already resigned from the Chamber of Commerce, of which he had been elected a member in 1832, because he considered that it 'was just falling into a political faction hostile to the Government'. To maintain his good name, he issued a writ for libel against the newspaper *Cernéen*, an organ controlled by his *bête noire*, Adrien d'Epinay, and he won his case.

That he cared not a snap of the fingers for a group so powerful in the island as 'the d'Epinay faction' is shown by the way he gathered a few friends together and established a new bank to compete with the Banque de Maurice. The latter had been founded by d'Epinay with the backing of some big English firms, and he did all he could to kill James Blyth's project. In spite of this, the new Mauritius Commercial Bank came into being in 1838 and received its Royal Charter in the following year. Up to the present time, an executive of the Blyth firm has served on its board of directors, and in its centenary year Mr M. Fortescue-Brickdale, the present Chairman of Blyth, Greene, Jourdain and Company, was its president.

CHAPTER THREE

The Thomas Blyth,
First of the Merchantmen

AR FROM bringing disaster to the plantations, the abolition of slavery had precisely the opposite effect. The Indemnity brought a new wave of optimism and Mauritius began to enjoy greater prosperity than it had ever known. More money circulated, folk lived more luxuriously, and the labourers now had wages to spend. James Blyth told in a letter home how even the consumption of French wines had become enormous, and added that the poorer classes were becoming too genteel to drink grog and their extra service money enabled them to indulge in a bottle of cool claret!

James Blyth had been steadily building the new firm into a substantial business house. He was trading heavily with Calcutta and was developing his interests in the four new settlements of South Australia. 'We have at least two-thirds of the New South Wales trade now,' he wrote in 1837. In the same year he reported: 'The American trade is coming into our hands as fast as it can.' Twice he planned to have a ship sent to Mauritius with instructions to touch in unobtrusively at Cannoniers Point and land a secret messenger with a large supply of money, which would be rushed to him in Port Louis and enable him to pay spot cash for sugar at what he described as 'easy prices', while the vessel would sail to Port Louis and there take on board the sugar which James Blyth had bought so favourably.

His active brain was ever devising methods that would bring grist to the mill. In 1835, he applied for the Mauritius agency of the Phoenix Assurance Company, of which a friend of his father's, the Francis Whiting already mentioned, was a proprietor. At a meeting of a special committee in London at which Mr Whiting was present, the Blyth House in Mauritius was given the Phoenix agency; and in the following year, James secured the agency for the Equitable Insurance Society of Calcutta, with authority to insure goods from Mauritius to all parts of the world.

Poop Deck of Isabella Blyth. Voyage to Mauritius.

The poop deck of the Isabella Blyth, *from a watercolour painted in 1852 by Lieutenant G. H. Gordon, RE, and now in Government House, Port Louis*

For some time, James Blyth had been hoping that they could own a fast sailing-ship which would ply regularly between London and Mauritius. The old *Amelia Wilson*, of which they had been part owners, had cost them £4,000 in repairs, and the London House regarded itself as fortunate in being able to sell the ship in England for as much as £2,650. On 19th December 1835, James Blyth wrote home that he had taken the plunge and had bought from Messrs Crook and Naz, their Seychelles agents, a fine new ship of 320 tons which was then on the stocks. For the sum of £2,000, the Blyths were to have her complete, with the exception of items such as copper and nails for her bottom. The ship was exceptionally fast and could carry nearly four hundred tons of sugar. She arrived in Mauritius on the completion of her maiden voyage from Seychelles in July 1837; and James named her the *Thomas Blyth* in honour of his father. This vessel became the first of a fleet of sailing-ships, all of which were painted a shade of yellow that earned them the sobriquet of the 'pea-soupers'. Eventually, over a period of years, the firm owned more than fifty of these vessels. The voyage from London to Mauritius in those days took between two and three months, sometimes longer, and the Blyths' 'pea-soupers' were designed for speed; their masters knew how greatly the firm's success depended upon swift passages.

Another project of James Blyth's was the formation of the Mauritius Steam Navigation Company. This he founded in the summer of 1836 with the object of running one or more steamships between Mauritius and Madagascar (occasionally touching in at Bourbon) to participate in the profitable bullock trade. James allotted to the London House the agency for the building of the steamship, the *Madagascar*, and he arranged that his brothers, John and Alfred, should provide the engines. To put a steamship on the water was then something of a pioneering action, for at that time there was not even a regular steamship service across the Atlantic; and the new enterprise called forth praise from many Mauritians, who reckoned that James Blyth was adding to the prosperity of the island. After an unfortunate delay, for which James Blyth blamed his engineering brothers, the *Madagascar* set sail from London River, steamed to Falmouth, where she coaled, then headed south to Madeira, where one of the Blyths' sailing-ships had unloaded coal that was to be taken on board to see the *Madagascar* through to the end of her voyage. With her bunkers full, the steamship set out for Mauritius by the Cape. James Blyth's instructions were that she was to 'steam through the calms' and use sail whenever possible, thus making her way to Port Louis. The *Madagascar* went into commission in the bullock trade in November 1838, two and a half years after the order had been placed for her construction.

'The trade in sugar,' James Blyth wrote in 1835, 'is now going into a different course from that which existed when I first came out. Then, almost all the crop went home on consignment. Now, more than half – say, three-fifths – is *bought* here.' For the planters it was a question of a bird in the hand, and London firms were now sending their own ships 'with hard specie to buy our sugars'. Most of the Mauritius sugar was then going to England, and as tea was becoming cheaper its consumption was bound to increase – and so was that of sugar. James Blyth was sending consignments also to Australia and elsewhere. His trade with India was steadily increasing. Estimating his profits for 1837 at £20,000, he wrote:

'The standing of our House in the Island has now assumed such a position that I believe it to be generally considered as the very first in point of solidity, extent of business, and to stand unrivalled in the enjoyment of public confidence.'

At the end of that year he announced the reconstruction of the firm, which then became Blyth Brothers and Company. The partnership with the Bettingtons had been severed four years before, and James Blyth now gave a share in the company to Benjamin Houghton, the clerk who had come out with him from England in 1830, and to another loyal servant, W. Danford. Amid the pressure of business in Mauritius, he found time to send home his comments on the progress of the parent firm in Limehouse:

'The more I reflect upon the losses we have sustained (in London) by our multifarious concerns, the more I am satisfied of their impolicy. . . . I don't doubt you will agree with me in my idea of concentrating our affairs as much as possible.'

He advised his brother Henry to put an end to ship-chandlery, oil sanding, coopering and other activities, and to concentrate on making sails and whaling-gear. 'That the warehouses of No. 45 (Fore Street, Limehouse) have been unprofitable for years is no secret from you. . . . You will do wrong to enter into any long-voyage whaling. It has never paid us 12 per cent per annum, which we can have here and less risque.'

James Blyth worked in Port Louis until the end of 1838 as vigorously as when he had landed on the island eight years before. His wife, Euphemia, had been compelled to spend two years in England for the sake of her health, but James had never left Mauritius for a day or taken a single respite from his labours. During those eight strenuous years, he had earned what was then reckoned to be a small fortune for himself, his father, and his brother Henry, and he set sail for home at the beginning of 1839.

Lieutenant Gordon's cabin on the Isabella Blyth, *from another of his watercolour paintings in Government House, Port Louis*

CHAPTER FOUR

A New Partnership

J AMES BLYTH had much to occupy his thoughts on the voyage. He had confessed in a letter home that one of his objects in forming the Mauritius Steam Navigation Company had been partly to provide a suitable post for Philip, whom he had made managing director, and he had given his brothers John and Alfred the commission to supply the ship's engines in the hope that they might receive other orders from Mauritius. Although the *Madagascar* had paid reasonably well on her first voyage, James had written to Bombay and Calcutta a month later 'to try in a quiet way to sell her to the Indian Government and thus bring the amount back into the coffers again'. One can picture his anxiety about the future of the Navigation Company with the unbusinesslike Philip in a post of responsibility; and his thoughts must often have turned to the future of Blyth Brothers and Company. He had described Philip's affairs as 'a source of unmitigated annoyance to me for many years', but the bankruptcy had been annulled in time for him to make his brother a partner with Houghton and Danford in the reconstituted firm. He had left them full instructions on how the business was to be conducted, and he was relying on Houghton and Danford to manage the affairs of Blyth Brothers and Company with the same success which he himself had achieved. He would fain have remained on the island a little longer to make sure that all would go well with the new firm and with the bank he had helped to establish; but he knew how urgently Henry was requiring his help in the London house, particularly in view of changes that were pending in its export trade.

Anxious as he was over these matters, James's first concern on reaching London was the health of his father, who had been ailing for several years. Thomas Blyth had relinquished his partnership in the firm he had founded, and at the premises in Fore Street trade was now being carried on under the name of H. D. and James Blyth. From Mauritius, James had been writing to his brother suggesting that the damp air

of Limehouse was probably doing their father no good and that the family home should be moved from Church Row to higher ground or even out to Epping Forest. The move was made from the riverside to a new residence, Park House in Grove Road, then in open country a mile and a half north of the Thames. There, Thomas Blyth died on 22nd April 1839, only a short time after James had arrived back from his long sojourn in Mauritius. He was buried in the family vault in the crypt of St Anne's Church, Limehouse, and on a pillar inside the church is a tablet to his memory. As executors of his will, he had named his wife, two of his sons (James and Alfred) and Benjamin Buck Greene, who had married his only daughter in 1837.

'I need not tell you, my dear Hal,' James had written home, 'how delighted I was to hear of the highly satisfactory marriage my Sweet Sister Bell was about to make.' Benjamin Buck Greene was then in partnership with his father, Benjamin Greene, a merchant trading with the West Indies. A few years later, the association between him and the Blyths was to be strengthened by permanent financial ties and was to enhance the status and prosperity of the Blyth firm.

James Blyth was now able to share actively with his brother Henry in the direction of the business in Limehouse, and three years after the death of their father we find 'H. D. and James Blyth' established as merchants and shipowners at 9 Austin Friars in the City of London. The wharf and premises at 45 Fore Street were by this time given up, and the Blyths had finished with sail-making, ship-chandlering and other activities that had been earning such meagre profits towards the end of their father's lifetime. Meanwhile, the two younger brothers, John and Alfred, seem to have been industrious and successful, for by 1843 we find them in business not only as engineers, but also as millwrights, boiler-makers and iron-founders at 57 Fore Street, Limehouse.

A little later, the constitution of the firm of H. D. and James Blyth was once more to be changed. This came about because, in 1846, Benjamin Buck Greene became the partner of his brothers-in-law. At least two years before the partnership was established, he and the Blyths had been jointly sending ships to the West Indies, and he continued for a time to trade with those islands from his own office at 11 Mincing Lane.

In 1846 James Blyth went out again to Mauritius to look into the affairs of Blyth Brothers and Company; and to William Lamb, the Master Mariner of the ship *Benjamin Buck Greene* in which he sailed, he left one hundred guineas in his will because Lamb had looked after him so well. Between 1847 and 1850, the *Benjamin Greene*, a barque of 405 tons, was making trading voyages across the Atlantic. Other ships of the Blyth, Greene partnership sailed to St Helena, to the East Indies, to Calcutta, and to ports in the Mediterranean. At the same time there was a certain amount of coastal trade, particularly to Bristol and Sunderland, from London River.

Right: James Blyth (from a painting in the London board room)
Below: Henry D. Blyth (from a contemporary engraving)
Below right: Benjamin Buck Greene (from a contemporary engraving)

CHAPTER FIVE

Mauritius and London

RADING WITH Mauritius continued steadily. There were changes in the firm there, too, and by 1850 a Mr Fernyhough was the senior partner. Active in the island's affairs, he was amongst those who strongly advocated the reformation of the Mauritius Chamber of Commerce and he became a member of its council. He was also a member of the first committee of commercial arbitration to be established in the colony and of committees set up to enquire into the bankruptcy laws of the island and to establish more suitable terms of indenture for engaging Indian labourers.

The eighteen-fifties were a progressive period for the island. Under the governorship of Sir James Higginson the planters formed a Chamber of Agriculture. Plans for improvements – irrigation canals, soil enrichment, better machinery in the sugar factories – were formulated; and as a result of these efforts, the output of sugar in 1858 was higher than it had ever been.

In 1860, Henry John Jourdain, then twenty-five years old, became senior partner of Blyth Brothers. This unexpected appointment was made by the London firm in the confidence that he would be able to solve difficulties which had arisen as the result of a dispute between the partners in Mauritius. Henry Jourdain was at that time paying his second visit to the island as the representative of Dreyfus Frères, selling Peruvian guano to the sugar planters. He now undertook a task before which many an older and more experienced man might have hesitated, and he handled it with success.

Fortunately, in setting matters to rights in Blyth Brothers, he had the help of an accountant, A. P. Ambrose, whose advice proved to be of the highest value, and who himself became a partner the following year. Indeed, his ability was such that a few years later A. P. Ambrose was asked to reorganise government finances in Mauritius.

Another new member of the staff at this time was Joseph Walpole Hollway, who had married and taken his bride with him out to the island. The couple had not gone by the long sea route round the Cape of Good Hope, as James Blyth and his young wife had done thirty years before, but had sailed as far as the north shore of the Suez isthmus, had crossed the hundred-mile wide isthmus on camels by the overland route, and had then embarked once more on a sailing ship for Mauritius. Thus there was begun the Hollway connection with Mauritius and later with the London House which was to last well into the present century.

As soon as he had surmounted the crisis in Blyth Brothers and Company, Henry Jourdain took full advantage of the trading opportunities that presented themselves. Hardware, coal, flour, fertilisers, textiles – these were among the many commodities shipped to Mauritius during that period. The discord in the firm was soon forgotten, and in a remarkably short time Henry Jourdain had made his reputation as a man of initiative and vision. Before he was thirty he was elected president of the Chamber of Commerce.

It was during his presidency that Mauritius became connected with the Cape by a regular steamboat service. For a long time the firm had been advocating the improvement of shipping connections with the island. Back in 1850, James Blyth had been asked as London representative of the island's Chamber of Commerce to approach the Secretary of State for the Colonies, Lord Grey, and put forward 'representations that this Colony should be made a port of call for one of the new lines of steam navigation vessels', and two years later steamships began to run regularly between Mauritius and Aden. The journey by Suez occupied a shorter time when, in 1864, Mauritius became connected with Marseilles for regular mail and passenger traffic by the Messageries Impériales, whose steamer *Baghdad* plied between the island and the Suez isthmus, while the *Emyrne* sailed between the northern shore of the isthmus and Marseilles, the overland route linking the two points. In 1869, on the downfall of Napoleon III, the line was renamed Messageries Maritimes and Blyth Brothers became its agents in Mauritius.

In the same year, the Suez Canal was opened. While this long-awaited achievement brought immense benefits to India and the East, business men in Mauritius forecast that Port Louis would suffer: no longer, they declared, would Mauritius be the 'star and key of the Indian Ocean'. Port Louis had been a convenient port of call for vessels on the main route to the East by the Cape of Good Hope, and this in itself had attracted money to the island. In addition to harbour dues from visiting ships (which the captains declared were excessively high and which were paid with a grumble), the vessels that had been damaged by storms had been repaired in the shipyards and essential stores had been bought in the warehouses. But now, since Mauritius was far south of the route from Europe to India and the East, the number of ships calling at the island must decline. Although the new canal reduced by more than three thousand miles the length of the voyage from Britain to India, it transpired that masters of sailing ships still preferred to go plodding round the Cape rather than risk a tricky voyage under sail through the canal, which was then a good deal narrower than it is today, and thus the loss was not at first so great as some had anticipated. But as the number of sailing ships decreased the port and harbour of Port Louis inevitably became of less consequence to the island's prosperity.

After the death of his brother Henry in 1864, James Blyth shared with Benjamin Buck Greene the conduct of the London firm, which in 1850 had moved from Austin Friars to 15 Philpot Lane.

As a man of business in the City of London, James Blyth had been making his way with confidence and skill. A letter he had written to his brother Henry from Mauritius gives us a glimpse of what he had hoped to achieve on his return to London: 'I shall be glad to find that you have been able to pave the way to our getting into some of the snug things in London . . . say a director's seat for each in a Fire Office, a life insurance company, etc. . . . ' Some of his hopes were to be fulfilled, for he had become a director of the London Assurance Corporation, which was playing so important a role in the development of marine insurance, and later he became the governor. Thanks to him, Blyth Brothers were appointed their Mauritius agents for marine insurance in 1864 and for fire in 1887; and he was elected chairman of both the Oriental Bank Corporation and of the East and West India Dock Company.

On the death of Lord Falmouth in 1852, James Blyth bought from the heirs the mansion house and large estate of Woolhampton in Berkshire. He restored Woolhampton church and later rebuilt Brimpton church in the hamlet of that name a short distance south of the river Kennet. His interest in agriculture and horticulture increased as the years went by, and the Woolhampton herd of cattle gained a wide reputation; some of those he bred won prizes at a number of the chief agricultural shows in Britain. He took seriously his obligations as an English squire, and he served as a magistrate for Berkshire. It was a far cry from the days when he had lived with his young wife in a cottage in Hackney before setting out to spend laborious years in Mauritius. To the regret of a wide circle of friends and business associates, James Blyth died on 2nd November 1873 at his London home, 24 Hyde Park Gardens.

Benjamin Buck Greene was seven years younger than his partner and was to out-live him by twenty-nine years. He served as a Public Works Loan Commissioner, a Deputy Lieutenant for the City of London, and for a time was Consul General for Paraguay. His career was crowned in 1873 by his appointment as Governor of the Bank of England, of which he had been a director since 1850. His London house was at 25 Kensington Palace Gardens (now known as 'Millionaires' Row') and his country seat in Berkshire was Midgham House with its pleasant estate. He became patron of the living there, demolished the old chapel near his house and in 1869 built St Matthew's Church in a position more convenient for the villagers. He became a Justice of the Peace and was High Sheriff of the county in 1865. His estate lay beside that of his brother-in-law, and between them they owned many Berkshire acres. In the later part of his long life – he died at the age of ninety-three – Benjamin Buck Greene lived quietly at his Midgham home, and on the day of his funeral it was reported that 'the tolling of the knell by Midgham Church bell was answered by that from the belfry of the sister church of Brimpton on the opposite side of the Kennet Valley.' Thus there passed a much respected man of business and country squire.

❋ ❋ ❋

In the year after the death of James Blyth, Henry Jourdain had returned to England to become a partner in the London House, which was then occupying premises at 3 King William Street; and the name of the firm was changed to its present style of Blyth, Greene, Jourdain and Company. Henry Jourdain's reputation in Mauritius had stood high; as well as president of the Chamber of Commerce he had been a member of the Executive and Legislative Councils of Government. Joseph Walpole Hollway, who had also been president of the Chamber of Commerce, soon followed Henry Jourdain to England and joined the London House, but before leaving the island he had introduced to the firm a valuable new member, Robert William Chamney, who had been for ten years in the Oriental Bank in Mauritius. The brilliant accountant, A. P. Ambrose, remained with Blyth Brothers, served four terms as president of the Chamber of Commerce, and in 1883 became a member of the Legislative Council of Government. When he died in 1901 he had been a partner of Blyth Brothers for forty years.

CHAPTER SIX

The Incorporation of the Company (1894)

NTIL the early eighteen-sixties, nearly all the sugar produced in Mauritius had been shipped to Britain. But when buyers in the mother country turned for their supplies to the cheaper sugar of the West Indies and to sugar made from beet on the continent of Europe, the traders in Mauritius were forced to find a new market. Most of their sugar was then shipped to India. So steadily did trade with the sub-continent increase, and so great were the numbers of Indian labourers on the island, that in 1876 the Indian rupee became the normal currency of Mauritius. Blyth Brothers and Company shared in this growing trade across the Indian Ocean.

Ships of the firm's fleet continued to make voyages between England and Mauritius carrying a variety of goods, including ironware and what was known as 'Blyth twill'. The cloth was stamped with the letters 'BB' and the company's trade mark, a wheat-sheaf with the motto 'Persevere' inscribed across it, which was the crest adopted by the Blyth family. Sail was, however, giving way to steam, and by the end of the eighteen-seventies the number of 'pea-soupers' owned by the firm had been greatly reduced. Rather than shoulder the responsibility of becoming the owners of a fleet of steamships, the partners had decided to charter steamers to carry their goods; and by the early eighteen-eighties, they were using only steamships for their foreign trade, while the old 'pea-soupers' went to sea under the flags of other owners.

Not many years ago, the directors of Blyth, Greene, Jourdain received news of the *Marie Laure*, described as the 'last but one of the Mauritius sugar barques'. She had been the sister ship of the *Thomas Blyth*, the first of the 'pea-soupers', and at one time had been trading for the Blyths between London and St Helena. About the middle of the century, the Blyths had sold the *Marie Laure* to an Australian firm; and after her life of usefulness had come to an end, the vessel had lain on the east bank of the river Yarra near Melbourne. The hulk of this gallant old ship had decayed until her back had broken and she had subsided into the river mud.

Of incalculable value to the trade of Mauritius was an event that took place in 1893, when the island was joined by telegraphic cable to the rest of the world. Always there had been a frustrating delay in the exchange of commercial messages with the markets of Europe, India, and elsewhere. As far back as 1870, Blyth Brothers and Company had urged upon the Chamber of Commerce the need for 'oceanic telegraphic communication'. One suggestion was that the Cape and Aden should be joined by an 'electric cable' which took in Mauritius. When the question was raised with the Government, the retort was that to lay a cable to Mauritius would be a 'costly luxury'. In London, Henry Jourdain did all he could to push forward the project, but it was not until 1893 that the cable which was laid to Seychelles linked Mauritius with the then existing cable system of the world.

The year 1894 forms an important milestone in the history of the London House, for then the partners decided that the time had come for the firm to be incorporated as a private limited liability company. The authorised capital was a quarter of a million sterling, and its predominant interests were to be those of 'carrying on the business of bankers, general merchants and commission agents'. The registered offices were at 41 Eastcheap, to which the firm had moved a few years previously from 12 and 13 Nicholas Lane, Cannon Street.

Henry John Jourdain was appointed chairman, and others on the board were J. Blyth Currie, Robert William Chamney, Henry D. Blyth and J. Arthur Gibbs. Mr Currie, a great-grandson of the founder of the firm, had joined it in 1887 and at the first board meeting of the new company he was appointed assistant-manager. Robert William Chamney, previously a partner of the Mauritius House, had left the island to become a partner in the London firm in 1889. Henry D. Blyth, son of Alfred Blyth and grandson of the founder, had become a freight agent and ship broker in the early eighteen-seventies. His firm had increased in importance when it became the London charter and freight agent of the large Japanese concern, Mitsui Bussan Kaisha Limited, a connection which still exists, and H. D. Blyth and Company still continue to attend to the chartering requirements of Blyth, Greene, Jourdain. Henry Blyth did not serve as a working director of the newly incorporated company; nor did J. Arthur Gibbs. Previously employed in the firm of Antony Gibbs and Sons, the latter preferred to spend most of his time in the country and in 1898 he published a book entitled *A Cotswold Village*, which has become a classic of its kind. He died in 1900 and was succeeded by his brother Antony Gibbs, who had been fighting in the South African war with the Royal Inniskilling Dragoons. There had been a long-standing connection between Blyth Brothers and Company and the Melbourne

The Sea Breeze, *one of the fleet of 'pea-soupers', from the original in the offices of*
Blyth Brothers and Company Limited, Port Louis

firm of Gibbs, Bright, who had for many years been shipping mixed cargoes from Australia to Mauritius.

Important shareholders who were not on the board at the time of the incorporation were James Pattison Currie and Fred N. Chapple; others were Charles B. Jourdain, an exchange broker of Calcutta, and Henry Montague Blyth. The last named, a son of Henry D. Blyth, went out to Mauritius and became a senior partner. He was forced to retire in 1915 owing to ill-health, and his death quickly followed.

In 1855, five years after Benjamin Buck Greene became a director of the Bank of England, James Pattison Currie had also become a director and he too became Governor of the Bank some years later. He had married, as his second wife, James Blyth's daughter, Euphemia. Since her brother Henry had died in 1862[1] and her elder sister in 1904, Euphemia was the oldest surviving child of James Blyth; and her husband succeeded as heir entail to the house and estate of Woolhampton, when he adopted the name of Currie Blyth. J. Blyth Currie, already named as one of the original directors of Blyth, Green, Jourdain, was his son.

In 1901 the death of the first chairman of the company took place. Sir Henry John Jourdain had married Ada, daughter of James Pattison Currie (Currie Blyth) by the latter's first marriage to Anna Dora Brett. He had had a notable career. He had represented in London the Mauritius Chamber of Commerce; in 1886 he had been appointed Honorary Commissioner for Mauritius at the Colonial and Indian Exhibition in London, and in the same year had been made Companion of the Order of St Michael and St George for his outstanding services to the island. He had represented Mauritius on the governing body of the Imperial Institute (now the Commonwealth Institute) which had been formed to give scientific and technical advice on the economic development of the national resources of the Empire. He had been a Deputy Lieutenant of the City of London and a Chevalier of the Order of Leopold of Belgium; and in the midst of a busy life, he had found time to serve as chairman of the Ocean Marine Insurance Company and a director of the London Joint Stock Bank. In the year before his death, he had been created a Knight Commander of the Order of St Michael and St George.

Robert William Chamney now became chairman of Blyth, Greene, Jourdain. He retained this office until he died six years later, when another of the original directors, Henry D. Blyth, was appointed in his place.

---

[1] The death of Henry Blyth had taken place in Australia; the young man's body had been brought back to England in a lead coffin filled with rum in one of the firm's sailing ships, the *Sea Breeze*, for burial at Woolhampton.

CHAPTER SEVEN

Expansion in Three Continents

I N 1895, shortly after incorporation, Blyth, Greene, Jourdain and Company Limited acquired the banking business of Benecke Souchay, and in 1900 the Acceptance side was disposed of to the London-Hanseatic Bank. Up to this time, the firm had been both Acceptance and Credit bankers.

Trade with Mauritius continued to be a major factor in the prosperity of the company. They regularly put one ship on the berth each month for the island and accepted general cargo through their loading brokers, Henry Langridge. This satisfactory arrangement continued until the Union and the Castle lines amalgamated, when Henry Langridge were appointed loading brokers for the Union-Castle Mail Steamship Company and could no longer act in this capacity for Blyth, Greene, Jourdain. But an arrangement was made between the firm and the shipping lines. While on the one hand Blyth, Greene, Jourdain agreed that they would cease to load a ship each month for Mauritius, on the other hand Blyth Brothers and Company were appointed joint agents for the Union-Castle; moreover, while Blyth, Greene, Jourdain retained the right to charter vessels to ship coals to Mauritius, they undertook not to ship any other goods in those vessels for their own account except in small quantities to complete a cargo.

Sugar from Peru was being handled by the company in association with the Peruvian Sugar Estates Company Limited; and because of a conflict of interests among various parties in Peru, this association unfortunately proved to be a source of considerable anxiety to the directors of Blyth, Greene, Jourdain.

The Peruvian connection had originated in Henry John Jourdain's early employment in the Dreyfus firm. He had become financial adviser in London, and had suggested that sugar estates in Peru owned by Madame Dreyfus should be taken over by a limited liability company. This was duly formed in 1895; and Blyth, Greene, Jourdain took up £1,500 in 7 per cent Preference shares in the Peruvian Sugar Estates Company Limited and became their commercial agents in London.

Soon more capital was needed for the purchase of machinery and developments on the estates, and an approach was made to the London Bank of Mexico and South America in the hope of negotiating a loan for £25,000. When this was refused, Martins Bank was approached, and agreed to advance the money under the protection of Blyth, Greene, Jourdain's guarantee and their signature to an agreement to extend for a period of ten years their agency in London of the Peruvian Sugar Estates Company Limited. The London House continued to advance money for the upkeep of the estates, and as part cover for these advances, Madame Dreyfus deposited £10,000 in Russian bonds; but even taking into account 'the sugar awaiting shipment at the coast or on the water', the balance owing to Blyth, Greene, Jourdain by 1897 was £25,000. Further securities, to the value of £10,000, were deposited in the following year. Financially, the Peruvian Sugar Estates Company continued to remain in low water; and by 1904 unpaid interest on advances together with commissions due to Blyth, Greene, Jourdain had mounted to nearly £10,000. The directors consented to waive payment until such time as the Peruvian concern would be in a position to meet these debts.

Madame Dreyfus herself was an unsecured creditor for £40,000, and it was agreed that, if she would accept Preference shares for this amount, Blyth, Greene, Jourdain would do the same to the extent of £10,000. This formed the basis for a contract dated 4th August 1904 between both parties and two others – namely, the Peruvian Sugar Estates Company Limited and the London Bank of Mexico and South America, which in 1902 had replaced Martins as the bank of the Estates Company. In this agreement it was stipulated that Blyth, Greene, Jourdain should be entitled to nominate a director to the board of the Estates Company, and in 1906 R. W. Chamney was elected, to be followed in 1907 by James Blyth Currie. The Anglo-South American Bank, which took over the London Bank of Mexico in 1912, were large creditors; and in conjunction with Blyth, Greene, Jourdain this bank bought from Madame Dreyfus in 1914 a First Debenture of the Peruvian Sugar Estates Company Limited for £25,000. Accrued interest and legal expenses had now reached the total of £40,000; and as there seemed little hope of a settlement being made in the near future, they brought a Debenture holders' action.

The next step in the record of the company's operations in Peru took place in 1917, when the Tambo Real Estate (part of the Dreyfus possessions in South America) came on the market. At the Bar of the Peruvian Court, the Anglo-South American

Bank and Blyth, Greene, Jourdain purchased it for a sum approaching £150,000. This estate was profitably worked for a couple of years and was then resold for £200,000 to Messrs J. Lionel Barker and Company Limited of Liverpool.

Trouble had, however, been brewing for Blyth, Greene, Jourdain and the Anglo-South American Bank. The Ordinary shareholders of the Peruvian Estates Company Limited, led by Madame Louisa Dreyfus Gonzales, had in 1916 taken legal action against them. The sum involved was considerable, and in 1936 the amount standing to the credit of the Tambo Real at the Anglo-South American Bank was over half a million sterling, the share of Blyth, Greene, Jourdain being more than three hundred and fifty thousand pounds. In 1948, thirty-two years after it was started by Madame Dreyfus, the struggle was terminated by the case being finally dismissed in the Supreme Court of Peru. At the Annual General Meeting of Blyth, Greene, Jourdain held in September 1949, the chairman said:

'I am happy to be able to announce that the litigation in which the Company has been involved and endured with so much patience in connection with the Peruvian Sugar Estates Company Limited, has been terminated in our favour, thereby freeing a considerable sum which, although convinced of the justice of our case, we had been obliged to hold in reserve against a possibly adverse outcome.'

In the opening years of the present century, the oil war between Marcus Samuel and Company and the Standard Oil Company was at its height. The Samuel brothers had established oil depots throughout the East; and early in 1903 Blyth, Greene, Jourdain started negotiations with Marcus Samuel to obtain the agency of the Asiatic Petroleum Company for Blyth Brothers, who had previously been importing oil from America. On 6th August of that year, the first consignment of kerosene, shipped in ss *Turbo* from Singapore, was received by Blyth Brothers at Mauritius; and by 8th September they had sold all of the thousand cases of oil. By that time, Blyth, Greene, Jourdain had been successful in obtaining for them the sole agency of the Asiatic Petroleum Company for both Mauritius and Réunion.

This consignment was followed by five thousand cases in October, shipped in ss *Euplectela*, and a similar quantity arrived in the following January in ss *Elax*. Although the Mauritius market was then stocked with no less than thirty thousand cases of Russian and American oil, Marcus Samuel and Company continued their relentless fight and gave Blyth Brothers and Company instructions to undersell the Russian oil and thus deter importers from shipping more, the object being to enable the Asiatic Petroleum Company to gain control of the market and obtain better prices for future consignments.

Foreseeing the great importance of a business association with Marcus Samuel and Company, Blyth, Greene, Jourdain encouraged their Mauritius House to give every support to the Asiatic Petroleum Company. Blyth Brothers carried out this policy with such success that by 1905 they were regularly receiving consignments of as much as twenty thousand cases.

On 20th December of that year, the formal agency agreement with the Asiatic Petroleum Company was signed in London by Blyth, Greene, Jourdain on behalf of Blyth Brothers. This continued in force until the end of the first world war and was replaced on 4th December 1918 by an agreement with the British Imperial Oil Company (South Africa) Limited, which became the Shell Company of South Africa seventeen years later.

The fiftieth anniversary of the original agreement was suitably celebrated in 1955 both in Mauritius and London by the companies concerned. It is of interest to record that Blyth Brothers and Company are today the oldest existing Shell agents in the world.

In 1904, the company was asked to become the London agent of the Anglo-French Textile Company, and the registered office of the latter was transferred from Manchester to Blyth, Greene, Jourdain's offices in London. This Anglo-French company had been formed in 1897 to erect cotton textile mills in Pondicherry, then part of French India, with the object of taking advantage of the preferential rates of duty in force within the French empire; but because of the inevitable competition with the textile industry of metropolitan France, the results during the first two years were disappointing. The Indian firm of Best and Company, which had sponsored the formation of the Anglo-French Textile Company, became the agents and managers of the mills in Pondicherry; and associated with Best in the enterprise were Baerlein Brothers and other firms in Manchester, as well as certain French textile interests. When Blyth, Greene, Jourdain became London agents of the Pondicherry project, it was the cementing of an old association with Best and Company, with whom the firm had long been trading in ground-nuts and other Indian produce.

In Mauritius, at the beginning of the present century, the price of sugar fell heavily. This was well-nigh disastrous – and not to the planters alone. To make matters worse, a cyclone in 1902 did a great deal of damage. The infectious disease of surra began to spread throughout the island and in the end carried off nearly all the horses and mules and oxen, so that there was a critical shortage of animals to transport the sugar crop from the fields. Men could be seen hauling cartloads of sugar canes to the factories. In this emergency, the Government made a special surra loan to planters. With this security, Blyth Brothers and Company imported thousands of tons of light railway material within a few months and the island soon became covered with a network of tramlines.

Joseph Walpole Hollway's son, John Walpole Hollway, who had joined Blyth Brothers in 1884, was senior partner during this difficult period; and when he went to London in 1907 to become a director of Blyth, Greene, Jourdain, he had completed twenty-three years of service with the Mauritius House. He had been born on the island and had spent part of his childhood there and was thus well equipped to understand local problems.

When the planters asked for a loan from the British Government in 1908, it was granted after a Royal Commission studied the sugar industry. A new Department of Agriculture was established. The sugar mills, which were now more fully mechanised than they had ever been, numbered no more than sixty, whereas in 1864 there had been three hundred. It was agreed that malaria could be kept down in Port Louis by improving sanitation, and in 1909 the municipality raised in London a small loan. This was handled by John Walpole Hollway, who was appointed the first agent general in London of the Municipality of Port Louis. In addition to financing the new sanitary works, the loan was used to help in the completion of electric light plant.

After two years' apprenticeship in the Bank of England, Henry James Jourdain, son of Sir Henry Jourdain, went out in 1909 to join Blyth Brothers. The failing health of H. M. Blyth, son of H. D. Blyth, compelled him to retire in 1915 after having been a partner for many years. This left as the only two partners in the firm F. J. Elyard and Henry Jourdain. The latter's partnership dated from the previous year; and it fell to them, and in particular to Mr Jourdain, to handle a number of important transactions that followed the outbreak of war – especially those relating to sugar and shipping.

The Royal Sugar Commission, established by the British Government in 1914, purchased the first 100,000 tons of the Mauritius crop and entrusted to Blyth, Greene, Jourdain the chartering of vessels to carry it. Shortly afterwards, because of the position of the firm in London, Blyth Brothers and Company were appointed by the Commission to look after its interests in Mauritius. In the following year, when the whole of the island crop was shipped to France and other European countries, Blyth Brothers became agents for the Hudson's Bay Company and the Bay Steamship Company which supplied the vessels to transport it to Europe.

Many Mauritians went to fight in the armies of Britain and France, and pioneers augmented the labour force with British troops fighting the Turkish army in

Mesopotamia. The British garrison stationed in Mauritius was withdrawn for active service, and the island was defended by a corps of volunteers. Since enemy submarines were taking a heavy toll of Allied shipping, it was vital for Britain to make the best use of all the cargo space at her disposal. Time was a predominant factor in sea transport, and in Mauritius valuable time was being lost in the handling of cargoes in Port Louis. It had been usual for a charter party to stipulate that one full day would be taken to load two hundred and fifty tons of sugar into a ship. It was necessary to speed up this rate no matter what it cost. Mr Jourdain obtained the enthusiastic and generous support of the planters, shippers, stevedores and dock companies. As a result, the loading rate improved to two thousand tons per day for each ship, thus maintaining throughout the war a turn-round that had never been known in the harbour of Port Louis.

Among the tasks carried out by Blyth Brothers during the first world war was one connected with the Japanese navy. Vessels of that navy were actively co-operating with the Royal Navy in the transport of troops from Australia; and through their close association with Mitsui Bussan Kaisha Limited, Blyth Brothers were appointed agents for Japanese ships of war which were coaled at Port Louis.

CHAPTER EIGHT

Changes in Mauritius

BY THE END of the war, the value of the sugar crop of Mauritius had risen far beyond all expectations. This boom continued only for a short time, but for a year or two after the end of hostilities it was phenomenal.

The Royal Sugar Commission found it hard to obtain sufficient supplies to satisfy the needs of the United Kingdom, and for the Mauritius crop there arose fierce competition. In 1919, as agents for the Sugar Commission, Blyth Brothers and Company were authorised by cable from London to offer the unheard of price of £90 per ton if they could secure ninety per cent of the island's crop for the United Kingdom. At such a price, it might seem that negotiations for the purchase of the Mauritius crop would have gone smoothly through, but there were planters who seemed to be convinced that they could get an even better price, and they withheld their crops. Eventually, Sir Henri Leclézio, KCMG (who, like his father before him and his son after him, was knighted for his outstanding services to the colony) succeeded in securing the acceptance of all but a very few planters. In this task, Mr Jourdain was able to assist decisively, and the required percentage of acceptances was obtained. As soon as it became known that the needs of the United Kingdom had been satisfied, the stranglehold of the international operators was broken and the price of sugar fell heavily. Some of those planters who had held out in the hope of obtaining a better price were also mill owners, and they found themselves unable to compete with the others for the purchase of cane except at a heavy loss.

The price to which sugar had risen at that time can be appreciated by recalling that while the value of the island's crop before the war had been 40,000,000 rupees, the value in 1920 was six times greater. Shortly afterwards, under the guidance of Sir Henri Leclézio, the Mauritius planters came together to form the Sugar Syndicate, through which the whole sugar crop has been sold each year to the great advantage of all concerned.

❋ ❋ ❋

The official currency in Mauritius at this time consisted of Indian rupees, the exchange value of which fluctuated according to the Indian rates. In the early nineteen-twenties, Indian exchange fluctuated so violently that Mauritius instituted exchange rates of its own. These differed so widely from the official Indian rupee rate that arbitrage shipments of actual rupees from Mauritius to India became cheaper than buying exchange from the banks. Blyth Brothers and Company shipped, on one occasion, as much as 5,700,000 rupees in specie to Calcutta on behalf of Blyth, Greene, Jourdain and Company Limited. This extraordinary state of affairs led first to the Government placing an embargo on the export of specie and finally to their introducing in 1935 a new Mauritius rupee pegged to sterling at one shilling and sixpence.

❋ ❋ ❋

During the first world war it had been necessary to grow a considerable quantity of maize in Mauritius to make up for the decrease in the supply of rice from India. But by 1920 the position had been restored. Blyth, Greene, Jourdain undertook the financing of large shipments of rice, edible oil and gunnies from Burma and India to Mauritius. At the same time, they were sending from Europe fertilisers, patent fuel, light railway material and many kinds of hardware. This business grew to such an extent that at one time the firm was consigning cargoes of these goods by chartered vessels from the United Kingdom to Blyth Brothers, sending ships in ballast to Calcutta and Rangoon to load rice and other items for Mauritius, and bringing them back again to the United Kingdom with sugar.

Unfortunately, the speeding up of dock and harbour facilities in Mauritius over which everybody had co-operated with Mr Jourdain during the war, was not maintained. Delays in loading and unloading ships became serious; even machinery urgently required in factories sometimes lay in lighters in the harbour for two months before it was unloaded. As a result, the Port Commission of 1921 was obliged to make drastic recommendations to remedy a state of affairs that was impeding the commerce of the island. The short-lived sugar boom was followed by a depressing aftermath. During the time of inflation, local traders had speculated in the purchase of goods, and many bankruptcies followed. Some of the planters had sold their estates at the top of the boom; when the price of sugar fell the new owners were faced with grave financial difficulties, and attempts were made to adjust the trade balance of the island by growing other crops.

Until 1928 Blyth, Greene, Jourdain and other English importers had been in the habit of buying large quantities of white sugar from Mauritius. This was good enough to go into direct consumption, and so much of it reached the United Kingdom from Empire sources under the preferential tariff that refiners were in danger of being forced to close down one or more refineries. This led to the adjustment of the preferential duties, which obliged Mauritius and other Empire producers to ship raw sugar for refining in Britain. Only a small quantity of white sugar continued to be made in Mauritius and this was largely for consumption on the island.

Since the economy of Mauritius still depended largely on the prosperity of a single industry, there were times when it was in so unsound a condition that financial help was urgently required. On several occasions Blyth, Greene, Jourdain arranged short-term loans involving large sums of money which were advanced during the inter-crop seasons. The sugar estates were failing to make profits because they were obliged to sell their produce so cheaply, not because they were badly organised. In the year that the island began to ship raw sugar to the United Kingdom, a Special Commissioner made an investigation of the industry and reported that it was being managed skilfully and economically. Sugar was in fact being produced in Mauritius during that time at a cost lower than in any other country, with the exception of Java and possibly Cuba. As a result of the investigation of the Special Commissioner, it was recommended that a loan be granted to the planters of Mauritius at a low rate of interest. This loan amounted to £459,600. Although subsequently the sugar crops annually increased, thanks chiefly to better cultivation and the use of more fertilisers, general prosperity did not follow, for the low price of sugar kept the island's finances in a precarious state, and it was not until the increased prices of the war years that prosperity was restored.

Henry James Jourdain retired from Blyth Brothers in 1931. Between 1915 and 1931 he had been Honorary Consul for Belgium in Mauritius and was appointed a Chevalier of the Order of the Crown of Belgium. He was a director of the Mauritius Commercial Bank; and in 1930, the centenary year of the establishment of the Blyth firm in Mauritius, he was appointed president of the island's Chamber of Commerce. When he returned to London he joined the board of Blyth, Greene, Jourdain and Company Limited.

The senior partner in Mauritius was now Mr Matthew Fortescue-Brickdale; and one of his colleagues at that time was Mr Reginald Michael Currie, a son of James Blyth Currie – and therefore a great-great-grandson of the founder of the firm. After leaving Cambridge in 1923, Mr Currie had served both with the company in London and with its Mauritius House, and in 1937 he finally returned to England to join the board of Blyth, Greene, Jourdain.

Mr Fortescue-Brickdale remained in Mauritius as senior partner until 1940. On coming down from Oxford in 1912, he had been introduced to Blyth, Greene, Jourdain by his uncle, Major Antony E. Gibbs, then a director; from 1914 onwards he had served with The London Regiment, was wounded in 1917, and after the war went out to Mauritius. He was elected president of the Mauritius Commercial Bank in 1937, and during his three years' tenure of that office the bank celebrated the centenary of its foundation in 1838 by James Blyth and his friends. For seven years Mr Fortescue-Brickdale was a member of the Legislative Council of the island, and in 1933 his public services were recognised by his being made an Officer of the Order of the British Empire.

CHAPTER NINE

The Malayan Establishment

OLLOWING THE DEATH of Henry D. Blyth, James Blyth Currie was elected to the chair of Blyth, Greene, Jourdain in January 1924. During the period when he was chairman and he and John Walpole Hollway were managing directors, great progress was made by the company. By the early nineteen-thirties it was in so sound a financial position that the directors decided that the time had come for them to extend their activities as soon as a favourable opportunity should present itself.

An opportunity for such expansion did arise in a most unlikely manner. It followed a casual talk in a railway compartment between Mr H. J. Jourdain and a business man whom he had not previously known. He learned that his travelling companion was chairman of Messrs Adamson, Gilfillan and Company Limited, a firm which had become so deeply involved in the failure of London buyers of pepper that the directors considered it to be no longer in a position to continue trading. As a result of this chance interview, a recently formed subsidiary of Messrs Adamson, Gilfillan and Company was taken over by Blyth, Greene, Jourdain. Thus it came about that the latter acquired an important subsidiary, Harper, Gilfillan and Company of Malaya.

Harper, Gilfillan's parent firm had its roots in Singapore as far back as the year 1867, when Gilfillan, Wood and Company was established there, at the same time as Adamson, Gilfillan and Company was established in London. In 1904, the London and Eastern interests were merged and Adamson, Gilfillan and Company Limited was incorporated in London with a capital of £70,000. The founders of these enterprises, William Adamson, Samuel Gilfillan, and H. W. Wood, were traditionally known as 'The Three B's' – Brilliance, Brains and Balance. After working for the Borneo Company Limited they had decided to go into business on their own account because they 'thought that the development of the *entrepôt* trade depended upon reasonable credit terms being given to Chinese traders in the outports'. At the time

S. Gilfillan Esqʳ
W. Adamson Esqʳ,
D. W. Wood Esqʳ.

Dear Sir,
The arrangements for a settlement of accounts between you and the Company being now concluded, I have been requested by the Board of Directors to take the opportunity of saying that they part with the most friendly feelings towards you and with sincere wishes (in which I cordially join) for the success of the Copartnery you are about to form among yourselves —

Your good business habits, great experience of Eastern trade, and honourable conduct, will, we trust, ensure to your new Firm a prosperous career —

I am, Dear Sir,
Yours faithfully,
William Leith
Manager

Letter from Mr Muhlinghaus of the Borneo Company to Samuel Gilfillan and his partners dated 2nd May 1867

when they began trading, Singapore was the main commercial centre for the Malayan archipelago and Bangkok and Saigon. Graded in Singapore and shipped from there, the varied products of these regions included gutta percha, camphor, timber, rice, sugar, cotton, tobacco, coffee, pepper, spices and fruits such as pine-apples and oranges. In 1887, the Straits Trading Company was formed by Gilfillan, Wood and a Mr Muhlinghaus; and it has been recorded that 'the relations between this premier tin smelting concern and Adamson, Gilfillan were of the friendliest: indeed, except for a short period in the 1920s, the senior of Adamson, Gilfillan's Singapore office was always a director of the Straits Trading Company.'

The first decade of the twentieth century saw the development of 'plantation rubber' as a parallel growth of the motor-car industry; and Adamson, Gilfillan and Company floated the Lumut Rubber Estates. This was their only incursion into rubber planting in those early days, for they did not then consider that East India merchants should be involved in it.

At one time or another, the original partners of the firm were all members of the Legislative Council of Singapore. William Adamson became an important public figure there; he was made a Companion of the Order of St Michael and St George in 1897 and was knighted ten years later. On his return to London, he became a director of the Peninsular and Oriental Steam Navigation Company and chairman of the Straits Settlement Association.

As merchants, Gilfillan, Wood and Company had imported goods on their own account, but later they held many agencies for such firms as Colgate-Palmolive, Heinz, and the Reckitt-Colman group. They also held agencies for various steamship companies. It was not until 1925 that they made their second incursion into rubber planting. That year, in conjunction with Eastern Industries Limited, they floated the Central Perak Rubber Company Limited and the Gopeng Parak Rubber Estates Limited. Since 1913, they had been associated with the rubber packing industry by accepting the buying agency for the Goodrich Rubber Company, and they handled a great tonnage each year in Singapore and Penang until the 1920 post-war slump brought this connection to an end. Thereafter, packing for various principals was carried on in Malacca, Kuala Lumpur and Ipoh, and is still continued today on a large scale. A development of the nineteen-twenties was the securing of the agency for Japanese cement manufactured by the Asano Portland Cement Company Limited. Between the years 1927 and 1939, as much as 250,000 tons was imported into Singapore and Malaya.

It was in 1930 that Adamson, Gilfillan approached the firm of A. C. Harper and Company Limited with the suggestion that some amalgamation of interests might benefit both firms. A. C. Harper and Company itself had been formed by the merging in 1917 of two private partnerships – that of A. C. Harper and Company and J. and Q. McClymont and Company. In 1886, Harper had been the first European trader in Selangor; he had begun to deal in horse fodder, but since he was then the only merchant on the scene he acquired the agency for the Straits Steamship Company at Klang, which was the seaport until Port Swettenham was built. He also was given the agency for what is now the Shell Petroleum Company. When he retired in 1907 share broking was the most important activity of the firm, and large profits were made during the rubber boom by the new partners, R. F. Grey, F. E. Maynard and H. A. Wootton. In 1918, however, this department was closed down as it interfered with their trading interests. In 1929, Harper acquired the goodwill of Aylesbury and Nutter Limited, who were established in Ipoh, Telok Anson, Taiping and Sitiawan. This firm was itself an amalgamation of the merchant firm of Aylesbury and Garland and of Nutter and Pearse, mining engineers. Such was the structure of A. C. Harper and Company Limited when the firm, under the chairmanship of Mr D. F. Topham, was approached by Mr W. A. Fell of Adamson, Gilfillan and Company, and there was acquired for shares the goodwill of the Adamson, Gilfillan business in Kuala Lumpur, Ipoh and Malacca. Adamson, Gilfillan took up 10,000 shares at par; and Harper, Gilfillan appointed them their representatives in London and wound up A. C. Harper and Company (London) Limited, their previous agents.

When a casual encounter in a railway carriage in 1935 led to Harper, Gilfillan coming into the control of Blyth, Greene, Jourdain, the company was thus acquiring an old-established Malayan firm of great repute. More than a century had elapsed since their first subsidiary house had been established in Mauritius.

Until the middle of the nineteen-twenties, Blyth, Greene, Jourdain had imported from South Africa large consignments of hides and skins, which were received in London for sale at auction. Before the sugar industry had developed in Natal, sugar from Mauritius had been exported to South Africa by Blyth Brothers and Company. In Natal this was sold, through the company's Durban agents, Theo Schloss and Company Limited, to local wholesale dealers and stores. A number of these dealers were clients of the company's export department in London and handled a considerable variety of goods from the United Kingdom and elsewhere. Long after South Africa was growing sufficient sugar for its own needs, Blyth, Green, Jourdain continued to trade with Theo Schloss and Company, and through them at one time bought large quantities of maize. With the same Durban firm, the company built up a considerable trade in wattle bark.

From India, the London House imported through Best and Company many consignments of cane jaggery (a coarse brown sugar) and ground-nuts; the latter commodity was also imported through Aspinwall and Company from Cochin. Trade in canned goods with Japan, which had begun during the first world war, was continued, although difficulties had arisen when the Japanese exporting firm suffered great loss during the rice riots that had broken out a few years after the end of the war.

During the inter-war period, Blyth, Greene, Jourdain also did a considerable trade in raw rice, which they sent from Burma to Poland, where it was milled. They entered this trade in 1927, when they shipped two or three cargoes to Trieste, whence it was transported to Cracow for milling by Messrs Wasserberger. Shipments to Trieste came to an end in the following year, when Messrs Wasserberger completed the construction of a rice mill in the new port of Gdynia, and they now handled all Polish rice imports exclusively bought from Blyth, Greene, Jourdain. The first steamer to carry rice to this mill was Messrs Glover Brothers' *Keats*, chartered by Blyth, Greene, Jourdain. The volume of business annually amounted to 40,000 or 50,000 tons, which was purchased from Messrs Steel Brothers, Messrs Bulloch Brothers and other merchant houses in Burma, and this trade continued up to the outbreak of war in 1939.

CHAPTER TEN

The Second World War

I was in the year 1936 that Blyth, Greene, Jourdain moved from King William Street to their present home, Plantation House in Fenchurch Street. During those uneasy years of the late thirties, many people were certain that if there should be a second war with Germany it would begin with massive air-raids on London. The directors made plans to preserve documents and records so that the company's business would not suddenly come to an end. When war was declared in September 1939, normal work at headquarters in Plantation House was largely suspended for a number of days while the staff of every department collected copies of contracts, letters and other documents. Ledgers were duplicated, and every evening those directors whose homes were in the country took the duplicates with them to places of greater safety than the City. This proved later to have been a wise precaution.

During the week-end of 10th May 1941, the offices at Plantation House, like so many others in the City of London, were heavily bombed. In the words of one of the directors, 'the only things left when we arrived on Monday morning were the safes lying on the floor on their faces – the plinths on which they had stood having been burned under them'. Because of the duplicates preserved in places of safety in the country, the firm was able to carry on business without the disorganisation that would certainly have been caused but for the forethought of the directors. Although current records were preserved, as described, the oil painting of the barques *Thomas Blyth* and *Isabella Blyth*, a work of William Huggins dated 1842, was destroyed, and the firm's archives, including James Blyth's letters and the private correspondence of the board with overseas companies, were in ashes.

One man who did not live to see the devastation of the offices where his influence had been so strongly felt was John Walpole Hollway, for he had died in the previous

Port Louis in 1842, showing the Isabella Blyth *arriving and the* Thomas Blyth *leaving,
from the oil painting by William Huggins*

February. His association with the firm was twofold: his father had served it for many years in both Mauritius and London, and he had married a daughter of a chairman of the company, Robert William Chamney. So great was his enthusiasm for work and so full was his devotion to Blyth, Greene, Jourdain that even during his last illness he was in constant communication by telephone with Plantation House. His death severed what could truly be described as a perfect business partnership with his chairman, James Blyth Currie – a partnership comparable in its harmony and success to that of the brothers Henry and James Blyth in the previous century.

For the remainder of the war period, the chairman's colleagues on the board were Mr H. J. Jourdain and Mr M. Fortescue-Brickdale, OBE, the latter having been elected in 1941. Mr R. Michael Currie, who had been a director since 1937, left on the outbreak of hostilities to serve in the army, first as an officer in the Berkshire Yeomanry and later on the General Staff; he retained his directorship and resumed active work with the firm after the end of the war.

The ten weeks' campaign in Malaya, which dealt such a blow to British prestige, ended in the fall of Singapore on 15th February 1942. Penang, where the most northerly of Harper, Gilfillan and Company's branches had been established, was evacuated on 16th December 1941. Taiping, Ipoh and Telok Anson had gone before Christmas, and Port Swettenham and Kuala Lumpur were lost very early in the new year. At Malacca, the last of the Federation branches was evacuated on 11th January 1942.

The departure from Penang and Telok Anson was so sudden that all records were lost; essential records from the other branches had been transferred to Singapore, only to be destroyed there when final capitulation occurred.

Almost all members of the European staff of Harper, Gilfillan were serving with the Forces; but fortunately, even as the Japanese were advancing down the peninsula, the staff succeeded in shipping a great proportion of their rubber stocks, thus freeing funds for immediate remittance to London. While they themselves were nearly all captured, their wives and families were evacuated safely; and since the company had liquid resources in London, Blyth, Greene, Jourdain were able to care for the families and other dependants for the whole period of the Pacific war. As this was known to the imprisoned staff, a great mental strain was lifted from them.

Five members of the staff tragically lost their lives. A. C. Gilbert and R. Darby, who were members of the Local Volunteer Corps, died on the Siamese railway. W. Brownlie, commissioned in the Royal Engineers, was reported 'missing believed killed' in action on Singapore island and has never been traced. F. L. Kennedy, a young Australian, reached Padang, Sumatra, but his subsequent fate is unknown. E. T. Caton, a member of the RNVR, was last seen in the Banka Straits, where his launch was burning and under shellfire from a Japanese destroyer. The other twenty-two were either prisoners in Changi gaol or forced to work on the Siamese railway.

E. C. H. Charlwood, the senior director of the company when the Japanese invaded the island, was given permission by the Governor to leave, on the grounds that, as a member of the Legislative Council, he could expect scant sympathy from the Japanese. To his great credit, Charlwood refused to go, preferring to remain with his staff. All who were with him know the outstanding example which he set throughout a period of imprisonment lasting for almost four years.

Before the war, the funds of Blyth, Greene, Jourdain and Company Limited had largely been used to give credit to customers abroad for goods supplied to them and in making advances to shippers against produce. But the exigencies of a wartime national economy restricted the export trade to priority goods; and in ships making voyages to the United Kingdom, there was little cargo space available except for what was necessary in the war effort, and this was purchased in bulk by the supply departments of the Government. Merchants ceased to handle the import of foodstuffs to Mauritius and private trading to the island was restricted to essentials such as fertilisers and gunnies, which were paid for largely in cash. Thus Blyth, Greene, Jourdain and Company's capital and reserves, which before the war had been locked up to a great extent in goods and credits, were freed.

The changes which were brought about in Mauritius because of the second world war were considerably more drastic than those caused by the Great War of 1914–18. The island once more became a prominent port of call on the Cape to India route. After the Japanese had captured Singapore, Mauritius became a base for both the Royal Navy and the Royal Air Force; a seaplane base north of Port Louis, and an aerodrome at Plaisance, now the civil airport of Mauritius, were constructed. Enemy submarines and raiders operated in the waters around the island; and to defend Mauritius against landing parties, a local force of coastal gunners and infantry was recruited. Two partners of the firm, Mr George Jeaffreson Miles Schilling and Mr Rupert Warren Knight, served as full-time officers in the infantry and later went with the Mauritius Regiment to Madagascar. The senior partner, Mr Hubert Reginald Ebbels, was thus left alone, and to help him Mr George Arthur

Robertson was sent out from the London firm. Throughout the war, Blyth Brothers acted as agents for the Admiralty, the Ministry of Food and the Ministry of War Transport.

During hostilities, Mauritius was forced to be as self-supporting as possible in its food. Although the planters were aware of the difficulty of growing food crops on their estates because of the frequent cyclones, they co-operated fully with the Government and gave up a quarter of their best lands. The results were disappointing; maize in particular could not stand up to the high winds that accompanied even a distant cyclone.

At the outbreak of the war, Blyth, Greene, Jourdain and Company Limited had been entrusted by the Government with the task of negotiating the purchase of the island's sugar crop. The London representative of the Mauritius Chamber of Agriculture at that time had been Captain Gustave Souchon, who had succeeded his father, Sir Louis Souchon, CBE, the first London representative ever to have been appointed. While negotiations for the sugar crop were in progress, Captain Souchon was called upon by the military authorities to undertake a special mission to Paris, and on his return journey he lost his life at Dunkirk. When the Mauritius planters were thus deprived of their London representative, they asked Mr H. J. Jourdain if he would act for them in the negotiations with the Ministry of Food for the purchase of the sugar crop. This request created an unusual position: for while Blyth, Greene, Jourdain represented the Ministry of Food in the purchase, a director of the same firm was being asked to represent the vendors. The Government, however, approved of Mr Jourdain's acting as negotiator, and Mauritius sugar was shipped to Britain without a break during the whole of the war.

In the years 1944 and 1945, Mauritius was struck by severe cyclones. This was a particularly heavy blow to the planters; and since the cyclones had reduced the sugar crop as well as the food crops they had been growing, it was clear that special arrangements would have to be made to assist them. Mr Jourdain was invited by the Colonial Office to visit Mauritius and confer with the planters and to report. He flew out to the island and returned with Mr Philippe Raffray, KC, CBE (later Sir Philippe Raffray) a member of the Executive and Legislative Councils. The result was that a grant of one million pounds was made to Mauritius by the British Government. Later, Mr Philippe Raffray succeeded Mr Jourdain as representative of the planters.

The French island of Réunion, 115 miles south-west of Mauritius, had found itself in a plight during the war; for in common with Madagascar it had elected to support Pétain's government of Vichy, and from France no succour was forthcoming. For nearly five years the sugar crop of that unfortunate island had been piling up until every gunny bag had been filled and every authorised storage place had been packed with sugar. All the spare rooms in the buildings around the docks had eventually been filled and still it was coming in from the factories. It was poured into houses through the roofs, and even the bedrooms were filled with it. The situation on Réunion became so desperate that the de Gaulle government in London appealed to the Colonial Office to ship the accumulating stocks of sugar from the island.

The question was raised whether much of that immense quantity of sugar had not so far deteriorated that it was not worth shipping. The Colonial Office asked Blyth, Greene, Jourdain for their help. The senior partner of Blyth Brothers and Company, Mr H. R. Ebbels, took a research chemist with him in the destroyer that picked him up at Mauritius, and together they inspected the sugar. After they had made many tests, they reported that it was in good condition, and in February 1945 nearly all the population of the port of Points de Galets turned out to cheer the first trading ship that had docked there for many years to take away sugar. The refiners who received it were entirely satisfied; and the experience gained by the remarkable situation on Réunion showed that, under reasonably good conditions, sugar could be stored unpacked and in bulk for a much longer period than had formerly been realised. Since that time it has become a general practice to ship sugar in bulk.

Although Blyth, Greene, Jourdain have never established a subsidiary company or even a branch office in the Seychelles, they have had long trading connections with this beautiful little group of islands. Ceded by the French under the Treaty of Amiens in 1814, Seychelles had become a British dependency of Mauritius, but in 1903 the islands had been given a new status as a separate Crown Colony. As early as the eighteen-thirties, Blyth Brothers and Company had been trading with Seychelles, and it will be recalled that James Blyth had bought off the stocks, from his agents there, the first of the firm's fleet of sailing ships, the *Thomas Blyth*. At various times, large consignments of guano have been purchased from Seychelles for shipment to New Zealand, to Africa, and to Mauritius. During the second world war, the company handled practically the whole of the copra crop of these isles and has dealt largely in essential oils, particularly in cinnamon leaf oil and patchouli, as well as in cinnamon bark, vanilloes, and tortoise-shell. Much of the success of the company in this area has been due to the loyal service of its agent, Mr P. V. Hunt.

CHAPTER ELEVEN

New Spheres of Influence

T HE COMPANY suffered a grievous loss in 1945 by the death of James Blyth Currie, who had served it for fifty-eight years and for the last twenty-one of them had been its chairman. His mother, Euphemia Blyth, wife of James Pattison Currie, had been a daughter of James Blyth, and he was thus a great-grandson of the founder of the firm. For the last years of his life he had been crippled with arthritis but had continued coming daily to the office from his country residence, Woolhampton Cottage, which he had rebuilt on a corner of the Woolhampton estate that had been retained when the property was sold in 1905. Neither his advanced years nor his disability had prevented his coming regularly to the City throughout the war, and it was while visiting his doctor on a September morning on his way to the office that he died suddenly. Devoted as he was to business, he had always been a countryman at heart. James Blyth Currie had never lost sight of the importance of strengthening the company's finances, and it was largely due to his success in this matter that the extension of the firm's business became possible.

Mr Henry J. Jourdain was elected to the vacant chair, and Mr M. Fortescue-Brickdale became joint managing director. The board faced a future in which it was difficult to discern the shape of things to come, with innumerable problems of reconstruction to be solved after the ordeals of a devastating war.

As far as Mauritius was concerned, the relatively high prices paid by the Government for sugar during the war had helped to restore the stability of the sugar industry. Previously, the planters had shown great courage in adversity; and at times when little help had been forthcoming from the British Government, they had been supported by merchants and bankers, whose assistance had taken the form of large credits for the supply of imported fertilisers, machinery, railway material, gunny bags and rice.

The granting of such credits had involved considerable risks during the nineteen-thirties when sugar prices had been uniformly low, and the directors of Blyth, Greene, Jourdain had not felt that they should tie up additional capital in direct investment in the island's estates. But now all political parties in the United Kingdom began to take a new and practical interest in colonial industry and agriculture. Immediately after the war, the drawing up of the Commonwealth Sugar Agreement opened a new era of confidence among the sugar planters of Mauritius and other countries in the Commonwealth and Empire. Under this agreement, planters were certain of being able to sell the greater part of their sugar crop to the United Kingdom at a price based upon the cost of production. Unstable prices had been the bugbear of the planters, and hurricanes and droughts had always been a lurking menace. With the Sugar Agreement and the institution of a hurricane and drought insurance fund[1] the two main dangers to the economy of the island were greatly reduced.

In these circumstances, owners of sugar estates felt that the time had come when they could with confidence incur heavy capital expenditure. The area under cane was extended, and the yield per acre was greatly increased by using tractors for deep subsoiling and the removal of boulders. Some of the smaller factories were closed and crushing was centralised at the bigger ones, which were enlarged and modernised. Between 1945 and 1960, the total number of factories operating was reduced from thirty-five to twenty-three, whereas the quantity of sugar produced annually was increased from about 330,000 tons to about 580,000 tons. All this required intense effort and considerable sums of money.

The firm decided to abandon its previous policy and to lend financial support to the development of Flacq United Estates Limited, an important merger of sugar estates which was then being negotiated under the imaginative guidance of Mr Fernand Leclézio. Now known as FUEL, it is the largest group of sugar estates in the island, and the success of the undertaking has exceeded all expectations.

Blyth, Greene, Jourdain also made a considerable investment in the Black River Investments Company Limited and Medine Sugar Estate, where important developments have been successfully undertaken by Mr Fernand Leclézio.

Established in 1830, Blyth Brothers had been operating for twelve decades as a partnership; but now the board of the parent company felt that the time had come for the constitution of the Mauritius firm to be changed. At the end of June 1952,

---

[1] The Hurricane and Drought Insurance Fund was to be of great benefit after the cyclones which struck the island on 19th January and 28th February 1960. The latter was the most violent ever recorded in the south-western Indian Ocean, and between fifty and sixty per cent damage to crops was reported. Apart from this, there was heavy damage to buildings, and about eighty thousand refugees had to be given shelter in the emergency. Fortunately, Fernyhough's Wharf, the headquarters of Blyth Brothers, suffered only minor damage.

the old partnership ceased to exist and Blyth Brothers and Company became a limited liability company wholly owned by Blyth, Greene, Jourdain and Company Limited. Because of the personal interests of the existing partners, and for other reasons, the change-over involved some complicated adjustments, but these went through smoothly and the partners became directors on the board of the newly incorporated Mauritius company. Mr H. R. Ebbels, who was appointed its first chairman, retired at the end of the following year after having completed a quarter of a century in the service of the firm, and was succeeded as chairman by Mr G. J. M. Schilling. The latter had been with Blyth Brothers since 1927 and had become a member of the Legislative Council of Mauritius in 1953. Mr R. W. Knight, who had joined the firm in 1931, was his senior colleague; and in 1954, Mr J. W. Jourdain, a son of Mr Henry James Jourdain, became a director.

Meanwhile, in Malaya and elsewhere in South Asia, the directors had been doing what they could to assess a situation of some complexity.

As soon as possible after the end of the war, Mr William Atkinson Fell, CBE, had been appointed head of the official Rubber Buying Unit, and in Malaya he had quickly organised delivery of rubber to the manufacturers, who had been obliged to use so much synthetic material during the years of conflict. The task of the Unit was carried out with great success, and Mr Fell returned to Britain in 1946 to become a director of Blyth, Greene, Jourdain.

It transpired that the financial position of Harper, Gilfillan was better than anyone had dared to hope. The directors felt justified in arranging for the firm to acquire the whole of the share capital of Mansergh and Taylor Limited, agents for rubber estates and tin mines: thus a valuable group of agencies was secured. Unfortunately, the political situation in Malaya quickly deteriorated and Communist bandits terrorised large areas of the country. This state of affairs continued for several years, and the troops sent into the jungles to destroy the terrorists found themselves fighting a sinister and resourceful enemy. At the Annual General Meeting of Blyth, Greene, Jourdain, held in September 1949, the chairman expressed to the shareholders the admiration of the directors at the way in which all connected with their Malayan associate were carrying on under extremely trying conditions. More than once, in subsequent years, the chairman was moved to repeat these words of gratitude and praise; and it was not until 1954 that he was able to report that conditions had so far improved that the work of Harper, Gilfillan in its many centres of activity could be conducted without fear of interruption by ruthless enemies.

The world prices of tin and rubber now remained at low levels, and there was little export trade with Indonesia, while political uneasiness in Singapore continued to give cause for anxiety; but in spite of all the difficulties with which they had to contend, Harper, Gilfillan continued to show satisfactory results. In 1954, by the acquisition of an interest in Pacific Traders (Borneo) Limited of Kuching, Sarawak became part of the trading territory of the firm's organisation; and in the following year, another subsidiary was acquired, Whittall and Company (Malaya) Limited, a firm operating as secretaries and agents for a large number of rubber companies. The successive chairmen of Harper, Gilfillan and Company Limited since the war have been Edward Clive Heathcote Charlwood, Frank Haynes Atkinson and William Herbert Crampton Bailey.

Carrying out their policy of expansion, the directors of Blyth, Greene, Jourdain decided to establish a subsidiary company in Hong Kong, and this they did by the formation in 1950 of the Plantation Trading Company. Through the new associate, a controlling interest was secured in W. R. Loxley and Company (China) Limited, a firm with mercantile connections and agencies in the East. At the same time, a controlling interest was acquired in Loxley's agents in the United Kingdom, W. R. Loxley and Company (London) Limited. The Hong Kong firm had been general exporters of the products of the Crown Colony and China, and had imported various consumer goods. They had participated in the agency work of the Edinburgh shipping firm, the Ben Line, and for some years had been their sole agents in Hong Kong; they have continued to be agents for the Japanese line N Y K. In the insurance field, Loxleys held a most important agency, that of 'The Royal', from 1919 until 1953, when the Royal decided to open its own branch in Hong Kong, while at the same time arranging for Loxleys to take the agency of 'The Lancashire'.

The firm had originally been started in 1870 by a young Yorkshireman, William R. Loxley, who traded mainly with the United Kingdom and Japan, eventually becoming one of the leading dealers in Chinese ginger. On his retirement about 1890, he sold the business to one of his assistants, J. Beattie, who with the help of two brothers extended its operations in general merchandise and opened branches in Canton and in London.

During the first world war, J. A. Russell of Kuala Lumpur opened offices in Hong Kong and Canton to deal with the treatment of Chinese wolfram and he appointed Loxleys to supervise shipments of this ore. In 1919 he took over Loxleys in partnership with his brother, D. O. Russell, and in the following year he bought also the firm of Perrin Cooper and Company, which had been established in Shanghai, Peking and Tientsin in 1900. On his death in 1933, Mr D. O. Russell acquired his shares in both businesses, and closed a number of branches in order to concentrate in Hong Kong, Tientsin and London.

During the second world war, Mr Russell was interned by the Japanese in Hong Kong, and in 1945 he resumed business with great success, assisted by Mr F. Meyer. When he decided to retire from the East in 1951 he sold to Blyth, Greene, Jourdain a controlling interest in both Loxleys and Perrin Cooper. Four years later, the Loxley interests were extended by the formation of the Alexandra Trading Agency Limited, a company created specifically to run the Colgate-Palmolive agency for Hong Kong.

For a considerable period, events in China and Korea had a restricting effect on trade in the Far East; but as soon as commercial relations with Japan again became practicable, Blyth, Greene, Jourdain resumed the importation of canned goods through the Nozaki Company of Tokyo.

In London, during the fifteen years that had passed since the end of the second world war, the company had been successful in expanding to a great extent the scope of the departments handling canned goods, essential oils and tea. Business in these commodities has been a striking feature of the last few years. The company has also taken a substantial share in Industrial Discount and Finance Limited, a hire purchase business.

In 1951, a change in the control of the Anglo-French Textile Company took place. The association of Blyth, Greene, Jourdain and Company Limited with this concern and its Rodier spinning and weaving mills had lasted for nearly half a century. Both James Blyth Currie and John W. Hollway had been on its board; and the former had served as chairman and managing director from 1925 until his death twenty years later, when Mr Edgar Baerlein had been appointed chairman and Mr R. Michael Currie had become managing director. In 1941, on the death of John W. Hollway, Mr Henry J. Jourdain had been elected to the board and was appointed deputy chairman in 1945.

All the shares in the Anglo-French Textile Company were finally sold to Best and Company and other Indian interests in 1951, when the conduct of the business was transferred to Pondicherry, and Blyth, Greene, Jourdain became European representatives. After the *de facto* government of Pondicherry had been taken over by India from the French in 1954, the sales of the mills' products in French colonial territories seriously declined; and in 1956 Blyth, Greene, Jourdain opened a branch office in Manchester under Mr S. Barker to handle the mills' European sales. They were by no means newcomers to Manchester: for they had previously operated there through agents to provide a service of maximum efficiency for their clients in the textile industry.

For some time, the company's business with wholesale traders and stores in South Africa had been expanding. This had come about chiefly through the influence of Bert Mendelsohn and Company Limited, a firm with wide interests in the Transvaal. The turnover was increasing to such an extent that in 1956 the board decided to form a subsidiary in Johannesburg under the title of Blyth, Greene, Jourdain and Company South Africa (Pty) Limited, with branches in Durban and East London; and similar developments in Rhodesia led to the formation in Bulawayo of another African subsidiary, Blyth, Greene, Jourdain and Company Rhodesia (Pvt) Limited. Both of these continue to operate with the parent company in its shipping interests and in its functions as a Confirming House in the Union of South Africa and the Federation of Rhodesia.

The Lonsdale Mercantile Trading Company, a subsidiary formed in 1956, are general exporters largely to the Middle East and North Africa and have extended the parent company's interests.

Another subsidiary, formed in 1957, is Glamorock Limited, a firm established to manufacture and distribute a type of wall and floor surfacing which had successfully undergone stringent tests. In due course, the building trade reported that this new surfacing material was proving of high value, and it began to make its way successfully in a competitive market. Glamorock Sales Limited was formed to handle the world-wide distribution of this new and important product.

CHAPTER TWELVE

The Company Today

SINCE THE end of the second world war, a number of changes have taken place in the constitution of the London board. In 1949, Mr H. Jervis Jourdain, MC, a son of Mr H. J. Jourdain, was appointed a director. He had had experience with Blyth Brothers and Company in Mauritius before the war, and after service with the armed forces he had returned to the island as a partner of the firm. Later, he had become a director of Harper, Gilfillan and Company in Malaya. Expansion of business had made it necessary to have another executive director on the board in London, and Mr Jourdain's personal knowledge of the work of the two chief subsidiary companies proved to be invaluable to his colleagues.

Ten years later, Mr Henry J. Jourdain retired from the chair but retained his place on the board. He had been associated with the company for half a century, first in Mauritius and then in London.

On 1st January 1959, Mr M. Fortescue-Brickdale, OBE, was appointed chairman of the company and Mr R. Michael Currie became joint managing director. Two additions to the directorate were made at this time by the election of Mr G. J. M. Schilling, who had been chairman of Blyth Brothers and Company, and Mr F. H. Atkinson, who had been chairman of Harper, Gilfillan.

While today the functions of Blyth, Greene, Jourdain and Company Limited as merchant bankers are of major importance, they and their subsidiaries are traders in a wide range of goods and commodities in many parts of the world.

In Mauritius, Blyth Brothers and Company export sugar, tea, and other produce of the island, while their imports include chemical fertilisers, Austin and Ford motor-vehicles, and building materials. They have been the pioneers of mechanical cultivation on the sugar estates and some two years ago celebrated the sale of the hundredth Caterpillar tractor. As has been noted, they are the oldest existing agents in the world of the Shell company; they have represented the Messageries Maritimes for a century and are joint agents of the Union-Castle and agents for many other shipping lines; and amongst the insurance companies they have represented, they have been agents of the Phoenix Assurance Company since 1835, of the London Assurance Company since 1864 and of the Guardian Assurance Company since 1886.

In Malaya and Sarawak, Harper, Gilfillan and Company with other subsidiaries export rubber, tin, ores and Malayan produce, while as sole agents for well-known manufacturing companies, mainly British and American, they import engineering equipment and general merchandise. They are secretaries and agents of many rubber companies; they hold important insurance and shipping agencies, and are Lloyd's agents for Selangor and Negri Sembilan. Through Loxley and other Hong Kong subsidiaries, the parent company is active in South-East Asia, while associated firms established in South Africa and Rhodesia trade under the style of the London House. By the end of 1960, the subsidiary companies numbered seventeen; and through agencies in different parts of the world, including Japan, the company's export and import trade has continued to expand.

Indeed, since the end of the second world war, in spite of diverse problems and uncertainties, the firm has grown more rapidly than at any other period of its existence. In the developments of recent years, there has been manifest the same spirit of enterprise that emboldened the founder of the firm to send his son, James Blyth, to establish an off-shoot of his London business in the island of Mauritius. The remarkable success that attended the efforts of the young man, both on the island and later in London, has been repeated in the expansion of the company's activities during the last decade. Blyth, Greene, Jourdain and Company Limited may be described as one of those 'family' firms which have helped to sustain the traditions of an earlier time in the mercantile history of the United Kingdom. Like other firms with similar traditions, merchant banking has become of ever increasing importance in their activities. A managing director of the firm and his son, James M. Blyth Currie, also one of the directors, are direct descendants of the founder, Thomas Blyth; the chairman is a nephew of one of the original directors of the company; and two other members of the board are a son and grandson of its first chairman.

Continuity of purpose has given the London House a cohesion that is clearly discernible during the last century and a half; at no period, during days of fair or foul weather, has it been other than resilient, enterprising, and ready to support to the limit its considered judgment. And in pursuing this steadfast policy, the company has advanced, in the City of London and on the African and Asian continents, to a consolidated position far beyond the dreams of the worthy Thomas Blyth. His descendants have built well and truly upon the success he won in the business he established on the Limehouse waterfront a century and a half ago.

Appendix

Companies in the Blyth, Greene, Jourdain and Company Group at 31st December 1960

LONDON

    Blyth, Greene, Jourdain and Company Limited
    W. R. Loxley and Company (London) Limited
    Glamorock Limited
    Lonsdale Mercantile Trading Company Limited

MAURITIUS

    Blyth Brothers and Company Limited
    Chemical Supply Company Limited
    Chaussée Motors Limited

MALAYA

    Harper, Gilfillan and Company Limited
    Whittall and Company (Malaya) Limited
    Magnetic Ore Dressing Limited

SARAWAK

    Harper, Gilfillan (Borneo) Limited
    Pacific Traders (Borneo) Limited

HONG KONG

    Plantation Trading Company (Hong Kong) Limited
    W. R. Loxley and Company Limited
    Perrin, Cooper and Company Limited
    Alexandra Trading Agency Limited

SOUTH AFRICA

    Blyth, Greene, Jourdain and Company South Africa (Pty) Limited

RHODESIA

    Blyth, Greene, Jourdain and Company Rhodesia (Pvt) Limited